world tour

Kenya

PATRICK DALEY

www.raintreepublishers.co.uk

Visit our website to find out more information about Raintree books.

To order:
- ☎ Phone 44 (0) 1865 888112
- 🖷 Send a fax to 44 (0) 1865 314091
- 🖥 Visit the Raintree Bookshop at **www.raintreepublishers.co.uk** to browse our catalogue and order online.

First published in Great Britain by Raintree Publishers, Halley Court, Jordan Hill, Oxford, OX2 8EJ, part of Harcourt Education.
Raintree is a registered trademark of Harcourt Education Ltd.

© Harcourt Education Ltd 2003
The moral right of the proprieter has been asserted.

Editorial: Sally Knowles
Cover Design: Peter Bailey and Michelle Lisseter
Production: Jonathan Smith

Printed and bound in China and Hong Kong by South China Printing Company

ISBN 1 844 21313 7
07 06 05 04 03
10 9 8 7 6 5 4 3 2 1

British Library Cataloguing in Publication Data
Daley, Patrick
Kenya (World tour)
967.6'2
A full catalogue for this book is available from the British Library

Acknowledgements
The publishers would like to thank the following for permission to reproduce photographs:
p. **1a** ©Picture Finders Ltd./eStock; p. **1b** ©Sayyid Azim/Ap/Wide World Photos; p. **1c** ©MP Kahl/DRK Photo; p. **3a** ©Sean Sprague/ Photo Agora; p. **3b** ©Anup Shah/ DRK Photo; p. **4** ©Joe McDonald/DRK Photo; p. **5** ©Rob & Ann Simpson/Photo Agora; p. **6** ©Sean Sprague/Photo Agora; p. **7**, **8** ©Hulton Archive; p. **8** ©AFP/ CORBIS; p. **13a** ©Paul Almasy/CORBIS; p. **13b** © Chinch Gryniewicz/ Ecoscene/ CORBIS; p. **14** ©Anup Shah/DRK Photo; p. **15a** ©A&M Shah/Animals Animals; p. **15b** John Gerlach/ Animals Animals © p. **16** ©Hubertus Kanus/ SuperStock; p. **18** ©Suzanne Murphy-Larronde; p. **19** ©Hubertus Kanus/ SuperStock; p. **20** ©Rick Edwards/Animals Animals; p. **21a** ©Mahoj Shah/DRK Photo; p. **21b** IFA Bilderteam/ eStock; p. **23** ©M.P. Kahl/DRK Photo; p. **25a** ©Giorgio Nimatallah/ SuperStock; p. **25b** ©Pictor/ Uniphoto; p. **27a** ©Jason Laure; p. **27b** ©eStock; p. **28** ©Sean Sprague/Photo Agora; p. **29** ©Ian Hodgson/ Reuters/ TimePix; p. **31a** ©George J. Sanker/DRK Photo; p. **31b** ©Suzanne Murphy-Larronde; p. **33** ©Charles Graham/ eStock; p. **34** ©Jason Laure; p. **35** ©Burke/ Triolo Productions/ Food Pix; p. **37a** ©Jason Laure; p. **37b** Rick Edwards/Animals Animals; p. **39a** ©TC Nature/Animals Animals; p. **39b** ©Jason Laure; p. **40** ©Sayyid Azim/AP/Wide World Photos; p. **41** ©Ben Radford/Allsport; p. **42** ©Hubertus Kanus/SuperStock; p. **43b** ©Anup Shah/ DRK Photo; p. **43c** ©Jason Laure; p. **44a** ©Joel Page/AP/Wide World Photos; p. **44b** ©Hulton Archive; p. **44c** ©AP/Wide World Photos.

Cover photography: Background: Getty Images/Taxi/Lee Foster. Foreground: Corbis/Torleif Svensson

Contents

Welcome to Kenya

Kenya is one of the most vibrant and diverse countries in Africa and has beautiful landscapes, bustling marketplaces, a rich history and fascinating people. Many visitors come to Kenya to see the amazing wildlife. There are hundreds of interesting species that can be seen on a safari.

Reader's tips

• Use the table of contents

In this kind of book, some sections may interest you more than others. Have a look at the table of contents and start with the chapters that interest you.

• Use the glossary

As you read this book, you may notice that some words appear in **bold** print. Look up bold words in the glossary. It will help you learn what they mean.

• Use the index

If you are looking for certain information on Kenya, then go to the index. There you will find a list of all the subjects covered in the book.

▲ **AMBOSELI NATIONAL PARK**
The open plains of Kenya offer perfect grazing lands for zebras.

Kenya's past

Kenya's history is a long and fascinating one, spanning everything from ancient tribes and slavery, to violent civil wars and modern businesses. Learning about Kenya's past is the best way to understand all the places you visit.

Ancient history

In the land surrounding Kenya's Lake Turkana, scientists found a human skull that was nearly two million years old. In fact, it was from a **pre-human**, called *Homo habilis*, who had a brain about half the size of modern-day humans. Our direct ancestors settled in Kenya much later – about 3000 years ago. These early settlers are relatives of the people who live in Kenya today. They include the Bantu, the Somalis and the Luo.

Around the 8th century AD, a new wave of settlers came to Kenya. They were Arabs from the Middle East.

The Arab settlers **founded** trading colonies along Kenya's coastline on the Indian Ocean. These merchants kept excellent records which tell us almost everything we know about Africa's early history.

◄ IN KERICHKO
Tea is one of Kenya's biggest exports. Picking tea leaves is hard work and takes long hours under the hot Kenyan sun.

Arrival of the Europeans

The Portuguese were the first Europeans to come to Kenya. The famous Portuguese explorer Vasco da Gama arrived in 1498 and before long, Portuguese merchants followed. In the 1700s, Arabs reclaimed their old trading ground and settled for the next hundred years or so.

The Kenyan coastline continued to bustle with **trade**. In 1895, the British declared total ownership and control of the area. They built railways, erected shipyards and established new trade routes.

The British also did a great deal of exploring. Many scientists had spent a long time trying to find out where the source of the river Nile was. British explorer John Hanning Speke found the answer. In 1858, Speke discovered that the Nile's waters begin in Lake Victoria. You can find out more about Lake Victoria on page 36.

JOHN HANNING SPEKE ▶
This engraving of the British explorer was done in 1860, just two years after he discovered that Lake Victoria is the source of the river Nile.

▲ **JOMO KENYATTA**
Jomo Kenyatta waves to cheering crowds during an Independence Day celebration in 1963. He led Kenya's fight for independence from Great Britain.

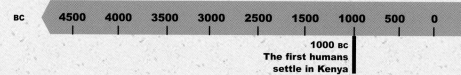

BC   4500   4000   3500   3000   2500   1500   1000   500   0

1000 BC
The first humans
settle in Kenya

Independence

In the 1950s, **native** Africans started a movement to end **colonial** rule. It was called the Mau Mau movement.

A man called Jomo Kenyatta led the fight against Britain. The battle for Kenya's freedom was long and bloody. Its most violent period was between 1953 and 1959, when nearly 14,000 people were killed in the fighting and the British imprisoned Jomo Kenyatta. In 1960, Britain agreed to give Kenya its **independence**, then in 1961 Kenya held its first free election. Eventually, the British released Jomo Kenyatta and he was voted Kenya's prime minister in 1963.

Modern Kenya

Kenyatta ruled Kenya from 1963 to 1978. He focused on helping the **economy** so that businesses boomed. He wanted to make sure that people had good jobs.

Daniel arap Moi took over after Jomo Kenyatta's death in 1978 and he has held power ever since. Rebuilding a nation is difficult, especially after years of foreign rule, but Kenya has managed better than most.

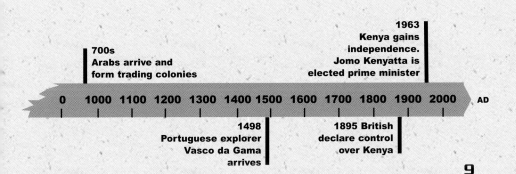

700s
Arabs arrive and form trading colonies

1963
Kenya gains independence. Jomo Kenyatta is elected prime minister

0   1000 1100 1200 1300 1400 1500 1600 1700 1800 1900 2000   AD

1498
Portuguese explorer Vasco da Gama arrives

1895 British declare control over Kenya

A look at Kenya's geography

Kenya has beautiful countryside. Tall mountains tower next to open plains. Sandy beaches stretch along rugged coastlines. With so much to see, this country is an exciting place to visit.

The land

Most of Kenya is covered by bush – a wilderness of dry, flat land. This type of **environment** is very harsh and low thorn bushes are some of the only plants that can grow well here. The bush lies mainly in the northern and western parts of the country.

Mountain ranges and highlands cover south-western Kenya. Mount Kenya is the country's highest mountain. At 5199 metres, it is also the second-highest mountain in the whole of Africa.

The Great Rift Valley runs through the middle of Kenya. This enormous valley starts in Syria (far to the north in the Middle East) and extends into the nations to the south of Kenya. Most of the Valley is 100 kilometres wide, with cliffs up to 1830 metres (6232 feet) high.

KENYA'S SIZE ▶
Kenya covers an area
of about 582,646 sq
km (224,961 sq
miles). Kenya borders
several countries
including Ethiopia,
Somalia, Tanzania,
Uganda and Sudan.

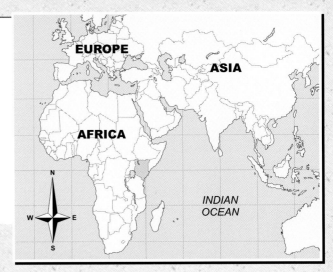

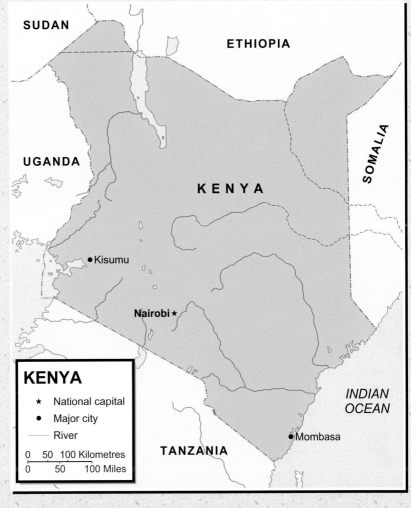

KENYA

★ National capital
● Major city
— River

0   50   100 Kilometres
0   50   100 Miles

Water

Kenya is home to Lake Victoria, the second-largest freshwater lake in the world. The lake crosses the borders into Tanzania and Uganda and measures nearly 70,000 square kilometres (27,000 square miles). It is just a little smaller than Lake Superior in North America. Lake Victoria is home to countless **species** of animals and plants. It is also the main source of the river Nile.

In the north, Kenya has another huge lake, Lake Turkana. It lies in the middle of the Great Rift Valley. It covers almost 6500 square kilometres (2,500 square miles) and is an important habitat for plants and animals.

Kenya's coastline is in the south-east. It extends for more than 480 kilometres (300 miles) along the Indian Ocean. The Portuguese explorer Vasco Da Gama first landed here and opened Kenya to many settlers from all over Europe.

KENYA

★ National capital
— River
▲ Mountain

Lake Turkana

Suam
Turkwel
Great Rift Valley
Nzoia
Ewaso Ng'iro
Lak Bor
Lak Dera
▲ Mount Kenya
Lake Victoria
Masai Mara National Reserve
Nairobi ★
Athi
Tana
Tsavo
Galana
Lamu Island

INDIAN OCEAN

▲ LAKE VICTORIA
This beautiful lake is the source of the world's longest river, the Nile. It provides water for people, plants and animals.

▲ CROSSING THE GREAT LAKE
People can take a boat across Lake Victoria. They can visit Uganda or Tanzania to trade at local markets or to go fishing.

▲ **FLAMINGOS**
Lake Bogoria is a good place to watch flamingos. They enjoy the warm water along the shores.

Weather

Kenya's weather varies. Kenya is on the **equator**, so some parts are extremely hot. On the coast, the average temperature stays at about 27°C. The highlands are cooler – temperatures there average between 13°C and 18°C. Rainfall also varies from region to region. The dry bushland in the north and west gets only a few centimetres of rain each year, while the area around Lake Victoria receives between about 100 and 180 centimetres of rain in a year – it rains there almost every afternoon.

▲ **HOT AND DUSTY**
A herd of wildebeest enjoy a drink on the shores of Lake Victoria. The cool water is refreshing during Kenya's hot and dry summer season.

NILE CROCODILE ▶
These crocodiles can live for 45 years and survive mainly by eating fish and turtles. But that does not mean they do not eat other animals – wildebeests have to look out for hungry Nile crocodiles too.

Nairobi: snapshot of a big city

▲ **NAIROBI**
In the midst of quiet rivers and vast plains sits the country's capital city, Nairobi. It has skyscrapers, universities and lots of traffic.

More than 2 million people live in Nairobi. The city developed around the railways the British built at the end of the 19th century. Today, Nairobi is a modern city with skyscrapers lining the horizon.

Lots of people think of Africa as hot, humid and covered with **jungle**. This describes some of Africa, but not all of it. Kenya's highlands are made up of cool, **fertile** territory, with plenty of wildlife, but not as dense as the thick forest that is often shown in films. Nairobi sits in the heart of these highlands. Its **climate** remains pleasant all year round.

The big city

If you want to see where Kenya's rich and powerful live and work, go to City Square, where the Kenyan government is located. There are several modern hotels and restaurants alongside the government offices. There is an enormous statue of Jomo Kenyatta in the middle of the square.

From City Square, you can see the parliament building. There are organised tours and it is sometimes possible to see the government in session.

If you want to learn about the history and **culture** of Kenya, head to the National Museum. If you like poisonous snakes, be sure to visit Nairobi Snake Park, right across the street. Many of Kenya's fascinating reptiles are exhibited there.

◀ KENYAN BAG
A handmade woven bag is helpful when hunting for bargains at City Market.

Shopping

While you are in Kenya's biggest city, you should look for a few bargains. City Market is an excellent place to go shopping. There are lots of antique stores, souvenir stands and second-hand dealers so it is perfect for finding interesting souvenirs. The Kariokor Market is another good place to shop. You may want to purchase one of the famous multi-coloured baskets sold there. You can fill it with picnic foods from the market stalls nearby.

Wildlife in the suburbs

Nairobi is just 8 kilometres (5 miles) from a **game reserve**. It is filled with animals you normally only see at a zoo. The reserve is called Nairobi National Park. It is the oldest National Park in Kenya. There are lions, cheetahs, rhinoceroses, zebras, antelopes, hippos and over 400 species of bird living in its 117 square kilometres. The rangers there are very knowledgeable and will help you find the animals you want to see.

The park has several picnic sites. One of the best known is Impala Hill. You can eat your lunch surrounded by beautiful scenery and try to spot some of the animals.

NAIROBI'S TOP-TEN CHECKLIST

Here is a list of ten things you really ought to do in Nairobi.

☐ Go on a tour of the Kenyan Parliament building. See if you can spot one of Kenya's National Assembly members.

☐ Head to City Square, the heart of Kenya's politics.

☐ Visit the Kenyan National Museum.

☐ Go antique shopping at City Market. Take home a piece of beadwork.

☐ Sample some Kenyan snacks at the Kariokor Market.

☐ Visit the Snake Park and discover which snakes are poisonous.

☐ Buy a bowl of ugali from a street vendor.

☐ Visit Nairobi National Park.

☐ Take pictures of some African animals.

☐ Eat a picnic lunch at Impala Hill.

▲ JOMO KENYATTA STATUE
This statue of Kenya's celebrated freedom fighter, Jomo Kenyatta, is a great spot to take photos. It is right next to the Kenyatta Conference Centre in Nairobi.

Four top sights

Kenya has a lot to offer. With so much to choose from, it is hard to know where to start. Here are some ideas:

Masai Mara

No visit to Kenya is complete without seeing the wildlife. There is no better place for this than the Masai Mara National Reserve. It covers nearly 1510 square kilometres (583 square miles) in south-west Kenya.

Masai Mara is home to many of the famous African animals, including lions, warthogs, rhinos, giraffes, zebras and many others. Visitors need to go with an experienced guide – and a powerful truck – because the animals here are wild and often suspicious of humans.

If you are looking for a sight that is unique to Kenya, head to the Masai Mara during the wildebeest **migration**. Hundreds of wildebeest move from one side of the park to the other every year in a large **herd**. They make a lot of noise and can be heard from a long way away.

◀ **A DANGEROUS CROSSING**
Trekking from one side of the reserve to the other can be fatal for many wildebeests. They may get drowned, trampled or eaten during the long and difficult journey.

▼ LIONS

Watch out for these majestic big cats while you are on safari. Remember that they are wild animals, and do not get too close.

ON SAFARI ▶

A guided safari ride is the perfect way to get close to Kenya's wildlife. These giraffes are used to visitors and are happy to be seen relaxing in the Masai Mara Reserve.

Mount Kenya

Mount Kenya is an **extinct volcano** and is a very popular destination for climbers. At over 5199 metres, it is the second-highest mountain in Africa. The top of Mount Kenya is freezing cold and covered with ice and snow. If you want to climb the mountain, hire a good local guide, or take a place on one of the organized tours. It can be very dangerous to go climbing if you do not know your way around. If you decide not to go up to the top of mountain, there is lots to see around Mount Kenya that makes it worth the trip.

Mount Kenya National Park surrounds the mountain. Be sure to stay with your tour guide. If you go off-track, you could end up face-to-face with an elephant or leopard. While in the park, there are plenty of other animals and birds to see. Some of the most common are baboons, monkeys, giant forest hogs, owls, hyenas and antelopes.

Most of these animals live at the base of Mount Kenya because it is warmer and there is a thick forest. As you walk further up the mountain, the forest changes from tall trees to bamboo. At the top of the mountain, it is very cold and rocky so only small plants such as moss and shrubs can survive there. Shrubs are very small bushes.

▼ MOUNT KENYA
The peaks of Mount Kenya tower above Teleki Valley. It is popular with mountain climbers.

Mombasa

Mombasa is the second largest city in Kenya. It has a population of about 691,300. A large part of Kenya's international trade takes place in this **port** city and Mombasa's harbours bustle with ocean traffic. In fact, Mombasa has been a busy centre of commerce for almost 1000 years. It used to handle much of Kenya's ivory and gold trade. Over the years, Britain, Portugal and Oman have controlled it.

Mombasa has a rich history. To experience this first hand, take a tour of Fort Jesus. In the past, Fort Jesus was used as a **military** and political headquarters. It is now a museum about Kenya's colonial past. It also has wonderful displays on the culture and traditions of the Swahili people. The Swahili people have lived in this area for hundreds of years.

Mombasa is also the perfect place to spend some time on the beach. You can swim, surf or even rent scuba or snorkelling equipment. If you go diving, make sure that you look at the **coral reefs** where there are all sorts of unusual fish and sea creatures. It is sometimes possible to see the remains of Portuguese ships that sank many years ago.

◀ MOMBASA
Larger-than-life
elephant tusks
decorate busy Moi
Avenue in central
Mombasa.

▲ PAST MEETS PRESENT
In the distance, steel skyscrapers rise above the
closely built modern homes of Mombasa.

Lamu Island

This tiny island lies off the northern part of Kenya's coast. It is the oldest surviving town in Kenya. It was one of the first settlements of the Swahili people and it is thought that the first settlers arrived more than 3000 years ago. In 1505, the Portuguese arrived. They discovered that Lamu was a useful port to trade from, and trade has flourished ever since. A period of control by Oman has left a strong Muslim influence.

Lamu is a special island. It has a rich history and most of the buildings are very old. In fact, many were built over 200 years ago. The streets are narrow and quiet because there are no cars or motorcycles. The only travel is by foot and donkeys. The people on Lamu Island live simply compared to people in Europe.

Tourists are drawn to Lamu Island from all over the world. It is a great place to relax and take a ride on a dhow, a small boat. You could also go fishing. Many of the locals make a living that way. If you really want to relax, you can enjoy Lamu's beaches. They are the island's main attraction.

If you have time to explore the island, start with the Lamu Museum. It has some great exhibits on Swahili culture and historical **artefacts**, including some ancient model dhows. There are also **ruins** to explore, including the Lamu Fort which dates back to 1821.

DHOWS ▶

Dhows are small boats. They take people between Lamu Island and the quiet beaches of Shela.

▼ ARRIVING AT LAMU ISLAND

Lamu Island is famous for its historic sites. Visitors go from port to port by dhow or by larger motorboat.

Going to school in Kenya

Many Kenyan children go to *harambee* schools. Harambee means 'pulling together'. People contribute what money they can and donate resources like paper, pencils and so on. If someone knows something important, like traditional history or wood carving, they might teach a class. Harambee schools started because there were not enough schools. The government did not have the **funds**.

Kenya has government-run schools as well. There is no law that says that children have to go to school, but about 80 per cent do get some primary schooling. Only about 25 per cent stay on to secondary school.

Children in Kenyan schools learn mostly in Swahili, the official language of Kenya. (English is the second language in Kenya.) They study subjects such as maths, science and social studies.

▲ **AT SCHOOL IN KENYA**
These boys are working hard at their local harambee school. Harambee means 'pulling together' – local people share their expert knowledge with the students.

Kenyan sports

Football is probably the most popular sport in Kenya, but Kenyans play all sorts of other sports as well.

When the British governed Kenya, they introduced the game of cricket, and this game is still played here. Kenya is also famous for its long-distance runners. Kenyan runners have won many of the major races and **marathons** around the world, including the London and New York marathons. They have also done well at the Olympics. Over the years, Kenyans have won gold medals in almost every long-distance event. Running is very popular with young people. You will often see people running along roads and through parks.

CRICKET ▶
The British introduced cricket to Kenya in 1896. It is still a popular game here.

From farming to factories

Farming is very important in Kenya. Kenyan farmers grow food crops like maize and sugar. However, tea and coffee are the most important crops grown in Kenya. They are sold around the world. Next time you are in a café or supermarket, look and see if there is Kenyan coffee for sale.

Not everyone in Kenya works on the farms. Many Kenyans work in factories making everything from medicine to shoes. Some Kenyans work in mines digging for rubies, gold and salt. Many people work in jobs that keep the country running smoothly, as doctors, lawyers, teachers and engineers.

Kenyan people are paid in shillings, which is the Kenyan **currency**. One shilling equals 100 Kenyan cents. If you travel to Kenya, you will pay for things using shillings.

Tourism is one of the biggest industries in Kenya. **Safaris** are the most popular tourist attraction. A safari is a trip into the African wilderness. Coastal towns are popular with tourists and the Indian Ocean provides plenty to do for people who like the beach. Tourists also spend money on souvenirs, gifts for friends, and local art. Products geared towards tourists bring Kenya lots of money. This encourages some Kenyans to continue to make traditional crafts. An artist from the Masai people can make a good living selling beadwork to travellers.

▲ OSTRICHES

Ostriches are one type of bird you might see in Kenya. They are the largest birds in the world. Ostriches are farmed for their meat, skin and feathers.

◀ EARNING A LIVING

Tribal women often weave baskets to sell at the local market. You may see local people carrying baskets full of produce on their heads.

The Kenyan government

The Kenyan government has a president and a National Assembly. Elections for the government are held every five years, at the end of each term. Together, the president and the National Assembly form the Parliament which makes the laws in Kenya.

There are 222 members of the National Assembly. The president appoints 12 members. The people vote to elect the president. They also vote for the rest of the assembly members.

Kenya also has a system of local government. The country is divided into seven provinces and one administrative area. Each has a commissioner who reports to the president. The seven provinces are then divided into smaller regions run by local chiefs.

KENYA'S NATIONAL FLAG

The Kenyan flag has three large bands, two white stripes and a shield with two spears at the front. The black stands for the Kenyan people. The red represents blood. The green represents wealth. The shield and spears refer to the country's defence of freedom. It is also a symbol of the Masai warriors.

Religions of Kenya

Almost 78 per cent of the people living in Kenya are Christians. Christians observe the teachings of Jesus, which are written in the New Testament of the Bible.

About 6 per cent of Kenyans are Animists. They worship spirits and nature. Most traditional Kenyan religions believe in a supreme god. For the Kikuyu people, this god is named Murungu. Murungu cannot be seen, but his presence appears in things like the sun, the moon and lightning.

The Arabs and Somalis in the north are mostly Muslim. Muslims believe in one god and follow the teachings of Muhammad, which are found in a book called the Koran. Muslims make up about 10 per cent of the population.

Many of the religions practised in Kenya combine different beliefs. For instance, Christians will share beliefs with Animists and vice versa. This makes Kenya's religions especially interesting.

JAMIA MOSQUE ▶
Muslims, followers of Islam, worship in buildings called mosques. This mosque is the most beautiful in Kenya.

Kenyan food

Food in Kenya varies from place to place. The many tribes and foriegn settlers in Kenya have each brought their own influence on Kenyan food.

Kenya's main food is maize. Kenyans eat maize plain, in soup or mashed up in a mixture called *ugali*. Ugali is often mixed with other vegetables and different kinds of meat.

Cows are one of the most important food sources and the Masai people have been herders for centuries. Beef, milk and even cow's blood are a regular part of their diet. The Luo people, who live along the coast of Lake Victoria, eat lots of fish.

Kenyans like ice cream and also eat a lot of fresh fruit such as pineapples, mangoes, bananas and papayas which all grow here. Sugar cane is one of Kenya's main crops. Some people suck or chew pieces of sugar cane to satisfy their sweet tooth.

◀ PREPARING UGALI
Local workers take their time preparing ugali, which is made from mashed maize. Many Kenyans enjoy this staple food.

Kenya's recipe

CHAPATIS

INGREDIENTS:
280 g flour
180 to 240 ml water
$\frac{1}{4}$ tsp salt
Melted butter

WARNING:
Never cook or bake by yourself. Always ask an adult to help you in the kitchen.

DIRECTIONS:
Combine the flour, water and salt. Knead thoroughly. Divide the dough into four equal parts. Sprinkle flour on a clean tabletop or wax paper to prevent sticking.
Use a rolling pin to roll out each part into a flat circle on the floured surface. Then spread thinly with the melted butter. Using your fingers, carefully roll up each circle like a swiss roll. Then roll each into a round coil. Using the rolling pin, roll each coil flat again. Ask an adult to help you fry one coil in a hot skillet or frying pan. Fry until brown on both sides. Chapatis brown better in pans without non-stick coatings.

Up close: Lake Victoria

Kisumu

Kisumu is Kenya's fourth-largest city and is popular with
visitors to Lake Victoria. There are beautiful mansions,
wide streets and majestic public buildings here, yet this is
one of Kenya's poorest cities.

Some claim that the city is not the best place to view
the lake, but there are several nice areas in the town. There
is one spot which is called Hippo Point because it is such
a good place to watch hippopotamuses. There are also
many places see spectacular sunsets over the lake.

Wildlife

There are many places to observe birds near Kisumu.
The Kisumu Bird **Sanctuary** is the most important and
is home to lots of large and unusual birds, including
storks, herons and ibises. Further down the road there is
a pelican sanctuary. Visitors are free to walk around and
explore, as long as they do not disturb the environment.

Along the coast is Ruma National Park. This park
has many of the animals you will want to see while you
are in Africa – lions, cheetahs, giraffes and oribis (tiny
antelopes). This is a **remote** part of Kenya, so there
won't be many other tourists there.

The islands

The three biggest islands on Lake Victoria are Ndere
Island, Rusinga Island and Mfangano Island. Each will
give you a different view of the lake.

▲ SPECTACULAR SUNSETS
Find a nice, quiet spot in Kisumu to take in the view of Lake Victoria. As darkness slowly rolls in, this lake takes on a colourful glow from the setting sun.

▲ SADDLEBILL STORK
This long-legged bird is a graceful flier – and a loyal mate. Male and female saddlebill stork couples will stay together for life.

Ndere Island is a great place to see wildlife. There are hippopotamuses, crocodiles and hundreds of different birds. It is also home to swamp antelopes and lots of fish. One of the more dangerous creatures that you may find there is the tsetse fly. The tsetse fly is known to carry fatal diseases, including sleeping sickness. Visitors need insect repellent, long trousers and long-sleeved tops to avoid being bitten.

Rusinga Island is famous for its big-game fishing. You can catch some very big fish in Lake Victoria. Rusinga is the best place to do it. You can rent a boat or you can fish from the shore. The biggest catch is the Nile perch, which can weigh up to 90 kilograms. Rusinga Island became famous when a 3 million-year-old pre-human skull was found there.

Mfangano is the most remote of these three islands. There is no electricity or running water. There are no motorized vehicles – which makes the island very peaceful. People go there to escape modern life.

FASCINATING FACT

The tsetse fly is a blood-sucking insect found in Africa. It carries a disease known as sleeping sickness. Without treatment, sleeping sickness can cause death. Someone in the final stages of this disease stays asleep for longer and longer periods of time. That is why it is called the sleeping sickness.

BE CAREFUL ▶
This tiny little insect, the tsetse fly, carries dangerous diseases.

▲ **FISHING ON LAKE VICTORIA**
These fishermen make their living on the water. They will sell their catch at the local market.

Holidays

Kenyans celebrate many public holidays. Kenyatta Day, 20 October, is an important national holiday. It is named after Kenya's first prime minister. Kenyatta Day celebrates unity and Kenyan national spirit. Kenya also celebrates Independence Day on 12 December. It is the day Kenya won independence from Britain in 1963.

Most Kenyans are Christian. Christmas is one of the most important holidays for Christians. It is on 25 December. It celebrates the birth of Jesus.

Ramadan is the most important event in the Muslim calendar. It lasts for a month and falls in the ninth month of every Muslim year. During Ramadan, participants pray and fast, only eating one simple meal after dark.

In many parts of Kenya, people celebrate their harvests and the change of seasons with festivals that can last for days. They often include feasts, dancing, and competitions.

▲ **PRAYER TIME AND CELEBRATION**
Muslims fast and pray during the season of Ramadan, a time of spiritual reflection for Muslims.

Learning the language

English	Swahili	How to say it
Hello	Jambo	JAHM-bo
Goodbye	Kwaheri	kwa-HEY-ri
My name is	Jina langu ni	JEE-na LAHN-goo nee
What is your name?	Jina lako ni nini?	JEE-na la-KO nee NEE-nee
How are you?	Hujambo?	hoo-JAHM-bo
I'm fine	Sijambo	see-JAHM-bo
Thanks	Ahshante	ah-SHAN-tay

Quick facts

Kenya

Capital
Nairobi

Borders
Sudan to NW
Ethiopia to N
Somalia to E
Indian Ocean to SE
Tanzania to SW
Lake Victoria and
Uganda to W

Area
582,646 sq km
(224,961 sq miles)

Population
31,138,735

Largest cities
Nairobi (2,312,300 people)
Mombasa (691,300)
Nakuru (317,500)
Kisumu (268,300)
Eldoret (233,400)

▼ **Main religious groups**

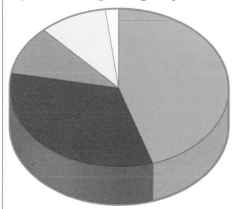

- Protestant 45%
- Roman Catholic 33%
- Muslim 10%
- Indigenous beliefs 10%
- Other 2%

Flag of Kenya

Coastline
536 km (333 miles)

Literacy rate
78.1% of all Kenyan people can read and write

Longest river ▶
Tana
708 km (440 miles)

Major industries
Small-scale consumer goods (plastic, furniture, batteries, textiles, soap, cigarettes, flour), agricultural processing, oil refining, cement, tourism

Main crops and livestock
Coffee, tea, maize, wheat, sugar cane, fruit, vegetables, cattle, pork, poultry

Natural resources
Gold, limestone, soda ash, salt barites, rubies, fluorspar, garnets, wildlife, hydropower

◀ Monetary unit
Kenyan shilling

People to know

◀ Catherine Ndereba

Catherine Ndereba is one of the best long-distance runners in the world. When she started running, people found it strange. Women runners were not respected in Kenya. But after winning several international marathons, Catherine quickly silenced her critics. She won a huge following of fans.

Jomo Kenyatta ▶

Kenyatta is a Swahili word. It means 'light of Kenya'. This is the name Kamau Wa Ngengi chose for himself. He adopted it when he began to lead the fight for Kenya's independence. In 1963, Kenya became a free country and Kenyatta became its first president.

◀ Mary Douglas Leakey

Mary Douglas Leakey was an important archaeologist. She was born in 1913. She moved to Kenya with her husband Louis to search for ancient human ancestors. One of her most important discoveries was human-like footprints nearly 3,600,000 years old. Mary Leakey died in 1996.

More to read

Do you want to know more about Kenya? Have a look at the books below.

Nations of the World: Kenya, Bridget Giles
   (Raintree, 2003)
Explore Kenya in detail, examining the history, geography, culture and lifestyle in this fascinating country.

Next Stop: Kenya, Fred Martin
   (Heinemann Library, 1998)
Go on a full tour of Kenya and learn about its past and present. Discover amazing things about its weather, land and animals. Find out what it is really like to live there.

World Focus: Kenya
   (Heinemann Library, 1994)
Learn about Kenya and understand the people. Discover how the real people in Kenya spend their time, what jobs they do, what school is like and what challenges they face.

Continents: Africa, L. Foster
   (Heinemann Library, 2002)
Read about Kenya and the other 52 countries in Africa. Discover all about the landforms, climate and vegetation as well as the people and animals that live there. Learn about the continent's big cities, countryside, famous places and much more.

Glossary

ancestor person's older relative who is no longer alive

artefact object that was made by humans in the past

climate typical weather in a place

colonial belonging to a group that has settled in a new place and taken over its government

commerce the way goods are bought and sold

coral reef ridge of rock-like coral found just under the ocean's surface

culture way of life and values of a particular society or civilization

currency type of money used in a country

economy country's industry, trade and finances

environment surroundings and conditions that affect an animal or plant

equator imaginary line around the Earth, halfway between the North and South Poles

extinct volcano volcano that no longer erupts

fertile good for growing plants

found to start or set up something

funds money set aside for a specific purpose

game animals that are hunted in the wild

habitat place where particular animals or plants live

herd group or flock of animals that stays together

independence state of being self-governing and not under the control of another country

jungle warm, tropical region densely covered with vines, bushes and trees

marathon long-distance running race over 42.195 kilometres (26 miles 385 yds)

migration people or animals moving from one part of the world to another

military nation's armed forces

native belonging by birth or origin to a place

port place where ships can safely dock to load and unload cargo

pre-human mammal with many of the same characteristics as a modern human

remote far away or hard to get to

reserve place where wildlife and land are kept safe

ruins remains of buildings from the past

safari trip people take to see wild animals

sanctuary sacred or protected place where one can find quiet and shelter

species group of animals or plants that has similar traits and can produce fertile offspring

trade buying and selling of goods

Index